THE CARDIOLOGIST'S DAUGHTER

Poems

Natasha Kochicheril Moni

Two Sylvias Press

Two Sylvias Press
PO Box 1524
Kingston, WA 98346
twosylviaspress@gmail.com

Cover Art: *Four Rooms* by Michael McDevitt
Cover Design: Kelli Russell Agodon
Book Design: Annette Spaulding-Convy
Author Photo Credit: Ronda Broatch

Created with the belief that **great writing is good for the world,** Two Sylvias Press mixes modern technology, classic style, and literary intellect with an eco-friendly heart. We draw our inspiration from the poetic literary talent of Sylvia Plath and the editorial business sense of Sylvia Beach. We are an independent press dedicated to publishing the exceptional voices of writers.

For more information about Two Sylvias Press or to learn more about the eBook version of *The Cardiologist's Daughter* please visit: www.twosylviaspress.com

First Edition. Created in the United States of America.

ISBN: 13:978-0692270714

Two Sylvias Press
www.twosylviaspress.com

Acknowledgements

Thank you to the editors of the following presses who first published these poems, sometimes in a slightly different form:

DIAGRAM: "How We Sketch the Departed," "As In Dutch, As In You," "In January   Our Rib Cages Are Cleaved"

Georgetown Review: "The Acupuncturist warns the Cardiologist's daughter"

Lifelines: A Literary & Art Journal from the Geisel School of Medicine at Dartmouth: "The Cardiologist's daughter contemplates a heart"

[PANK]: "Eight Years After, Pink Still Startles Her"

Pontoon: An Anthology of Washington State Poets: "An Exploration After 6,000 mg of Amoxicillin," "The Cardiologist Speaks"

Sierra Nevada Review: "Cranberry Sauce Provides an Improper Dressing for the Modern Turkey"

Silk Road Review: "Kneeling to Ganges"

SirenLit: "To Draw, To Smoke," "Reading My Mother's Words on the Path to My Cabin"

The 2River View: "Hold Fast to Mother's Spine," "After My Mother's Hip Replacement We Gather Around Her Heart"

The Other Voices International Project: "We Are Doing Rounds," "After the tsunami, we searched"

The Pedestal Magazine: "It wasn't like we were eating the squirrels"

Toasted Cheese Literary Journal: "We speak of water," "Massage School Translations," "On an Interview to Rent Space from a Chiropractor, I Discover a Mutual Admiration for Handling Skulls," "The Cardiologist, his daughter cradle a model," "The Cardiologist's daughter is concerned," "When I Approach my Advisor for Advice on How to Move Forward With Greater Ease After a Bumpy Start of Going Premed in My Thirties, He Performs a Well-Rehearsed Soliloquy"

Vox Populi, Seattle Poetry Festival 2007 Anthology: "In America, Auntie remembers Janaki"

Wicked Alice: "After Completing the MCAT and Before Returning to the Northwest, My Room Fills With Longing"

Zubaan Books (an imprint of Kali for Women) anthology, *Bittersweet: Decolonizing the South Asian Diaspora:* "When We Raise a Wall, We Leave Dixie Out," "In our family home we, like our mother's cuttings, will grow," "In Dream We Support a Two-Headed Tiger"

Special thanks to the editors of Two Sylvias Press, Annette Spaulding-Convy and Kelli Russell Agodon for their active support of my first full-length book. Passion, which governs their own writing and willingness to take risks on poets, in a time when the market is flooded with poetry, says everything about their substance.

Many thanks to the West Coast poets who welcomed me, offered encouragement, critique, and guidance: Ilya Kaminsky, Janet Norman Knox, Jeannine Hall Gailey, Jenifer Browne Lawrence, Lana Hechtman Ayers, Ronda Broatch, Holly Hughes, Tamara Kaye Sellman, Denel Bartsch, and Drew Kunz.

To those, whose instruction surpassed books:

Dr. Maryanne Wolf, who more than lit my brain on fire, but continues to inspire me with her reading and language research from afar.

Dr. Greg Yasuda, who guides my hands through listening, my head through unwavering patience, and my heart through laughter. He, who with no small magic, helps me build and rebuild again.

Dr. Mari Ellingsen who saw in me a spark and encouraged me to chase it.

Professor Sandra Banks, who gave me a solid base for my first year of medical sciences. Much of my success, I owe to you.

Dr. Rebecca Love, whose zeal for teaching gross anatomy in an environment that commands respect for the cadavers and the stories they carry, delivered me to a place of peace for this necessary learning.

Dr. Harold Modell, whose office I have spent entirely way too much time in, but has rendered me with a strange affection for this man who constructs models and programs that make me question more deeply.

Beverly Foote, my high school English teacher turned poet friend, whose words and spirit nurture me thoroughly.

Dr. Nancy Welliver, who in short time has helped me re-educate my heart.

Especially to my mother, Wilhelmina Moni and my father, Dr. Kochicheril Narayan Moni, whose practice is my greatest teacher.

Thanks to Michael McDevitt, whose art graces *The Cardiologist's Daughter* cover. Michael's visual work has inspired me for over nineteen years, so it is an absolute thrill to have his art alongside my words. Please visit his website (www.mmcdevitt.com) to view his portfolio, purchase his paintings, or commission him.

Thanks to those who have held the work of me in their open hands and persist as friends: Leslie Weisberger, Milo Redwood, Mari and Rod Mann, Rachel Schiefer, Bernie Donanberg, Quentin Benson, Pamela Dharamsey Lee, Eddie Williams, Matt Price, Emily Hilligoss, and especially the vivacious Kate Jaffe, the puzzling David Jaffe, and the indomitable Laura Murphy, who have offered me more than shelter—a proxy family.

To my Mills team: Lily Dashiell, Bianca Schilling, and fellow cardio daughters: Kat Moon and Radhika Snyder, who kept me in the game of premed.

To Anna Martin, at Bastyr University, who offered me immense support and friendship through the process of completing *The Cardiologist's Daughter*.

And to you who permit this detailed acknowledgment. Many have impacted my ability to realize this book (over the past ten years)—too many to thank. Thank you to you, too.

TABLE OF CONTENTS

I. *Where Heat Overflows to Heart*

II. *An Arc Toward Normalcy*

III. *Eulogy for Collapsed Structures*

IV. *Somewhere in a Room of Eggs*

for my R.N. mother, my Cardiologist father
who instilled in me a deep curiosity for learning,
a strong ethic, and a mutual love for the language
and practice of true medicine regardless of its origin

I.

WHERE HEAT OVERFLOWS TO HEART

The Cardiologist's Daughter Returns Home

i.

I was sleeping and she was screaming

and it wasn't uncommon

to hear screaming in the morning.

But it wasn't

clash. It was late

August heat and a man overdoing it

in the garden. Early morning heat

and a man dropping, hand

to chest among his

roses and if you must

know, that man

was her

husband—that man, her husband,

my father, he was

going.

But what I heard

was screaming

and I tried to roll

over and sleep.

I was going

to the mall with a new

friend who could have been an old

friend from school, now again in the same

school which was college and we were

going shopping, shopping for nothing

the way you go shopping when you are only

nineteen and your friend is eighteen

because you are home

and you cannot

shake your mall rat

roots. And who would prefer

the beach when there are so many

tourists, lying towel-to-towel-to-towel, spread

out like bread in broilers,

consecutive, ready

to crisp.

But I couldn't fall

asleep, even if no one was calling

to me about the spade that had fallen

in the garden, my father among his multi-

colored roses, my mother, the R.N., folding her Cardio

husband into the passenger seat, my father a fallen

father.

My parents. A Heart. A Spade. I made

the call to my friend, told him I heard screaming

I, now, knew my father

was on his way to the E.R.

but not to worry, my mother

told me *When you are ready*

drive down to the hospital, find us

and I should have known enough—

when my mother said *chest*

tightness what she meant was

M.I.

How like an R.N., how like a Dutch

woman, how like my mother, not to worry

a daughter and so I climbed

into the shower and with every beat

of the water began to realize my father

could—

my father, the Cardiologist could—

ii.

The brain is plastic, the heart (except

the model on my father's desk) is not

the heart is a little off

center, the heart will not be

easily fooled, although it may endure

reconstruction, allow a degree

of metal, the occasional

alternate reroute with vein

cultivated from medial thigh

the heart would rather be left

alone in its cavity, just the heart and its

pericardium, alone, multi-layered.

Neither heart, nor brain enjoy electricity

from shock, but they will comply.

iii.

My friend, not the friend with whom I was going

shopping, but my across-the-street friend, the one who introduced

herself on my doorstep ten years ago, clutching a bag of Mary-Jane—

Do you want to feed the ducks with me—this friend meets

me in the lobby of the second

hospital, the first one

good enough to deliver

the *Stand Clear*

and Shock

twice before my father

decided he wasn't done, didn't roll

over as I watched, not knowing

the smell that rose

was my father

flesh, electricity uniting—

iv.

It was Israel we reviewed in the lobby, frame

after frame of Israel. My friend had returned

and I ate her offerings, a photo,

a bite of candy

      —I broke down—

and purchased while

in the waiting

room strangers prayed

for my father, my mother—

among my friend's mother

the silence like water, it ran

over us and we parted—

v.

Quadruple. Quadrangle. Quadruple.

      Quadrangle.

I repeat and it doesn't

disappear.   The bypass cannot

      be bypassed and in returning

life, there will be death and

with it, tissue upon

      tissue blooming

      the rows as rose

a garden of flesh

raising a bed

      of stitches.

The Acupuncturist warns the Cardiologist's daughter

for Denise DuPree, LAc

her heart has caught fire, has swelled
        to contain too much
        heat, has jostled her kidneys

and failed them—two small pools cooling.
        Her heart will not release. The Acupuncturist
        suggests Asian pears, licorice tea.

A village where volcano misses
        ocean. A swim where water/fire
        wed without smoke.

The Cardiologist's daughter shuts her eyes
        to roofs caving
        and flame, so much flame—

her skull, a crucible
        where heat overflows to heart.
        And she thinks she is

her father, Cardiologist, balancing
        more than blood—
        so many people simmering,

reducing through her
        chambers. The Acupuncturist spells
        her message in metal.

Look, there are ways to warm,
        trace your path in water. Rise.

We speak of water

for Ilya Kaminsky

                and he raises

a glass   gestures

              with his free

                        arm as if a water

              fowl is being

raised from within

(this is California   Southern)

——*You must have water*——

I am filled   I might tell

              him of the many

nights I have been dreaming

of Fabergé   how dancing

on eggs   in dream   is more

              like floating

how floating   is more

like eating

down

plucking   feather after   (invisible)

feather   from one's throat

irritates   the esophagus

The truth is

I have been   speaking

to another

who knows   about   double

osmosis   He tells me   what

becomes   of fluids

before preserving   before   the viewing

about water   after water

where drains   in morgues

empty

how   California   is

        the great recycler

The truth is   I don't know this   yet

      The truth is   I am not

        thirsty   The truth is

always

     like separating egg   from apricot

Hold Fast to Mother's Spine

This morning she aches for a beach walk

      thin grain of sand below her

horizontal expanse where water animals emerge

      their bodies half-crescents, their movements

effortless. This morning they'll prove her disc prolapsed, pop

      the slide onto luminescent screen, slide their fingers over

runaway dorsal captured on MRI. They'll say surgery.

      She'll see an ocean splitting wave. They'll say nerve block.

She'll see shore dolphins, faultless backs cresting.

We leave the beaches for the tourists, mostly

wish the squids upon them, a baker's dozen casting bets over which

redhead, blonde exposed by sun, discovered the joy of burning

in places deemed ordinary at the beach. A blister of buns swelling

below a sundress marked *go Navy*.

                                        We leave the beaches for the tourists,

mostly because the scent of butter, flesh we reserve for the International

House of Pancakes, a plate of pig teeming with syrup-

flavored-syrup the kind that isn't anything but a woman

with a red cloth managing a kink of hair.

            We leave the beaches for the tourists, mostly

because we promised our mothers not to go

where Natalia was almost meal, one bull

        shark separating femoris

        from femur, an explosion   pronouncing

her wounded, widowed   at once

We leave the beaches   we leave our mothers   manufacture

gardens of sand   to turn   with miniature

rakes   force   our bodies

                                as narcissus   winter away

The Optometrist explains her eyes, especially

the right, how it has become
        lazy, the husband who relies on his wife's
        perception of what is/is not going on in their son's
        kindergarten. The left reading what the right ignores.

There are lines
spread in a circle. A test for astigmatism. A picture of a sun—
converging on a center of white.

> *Cover one eye and see how some spokes appear darker*
> *than the rest. If so, you may have*
> *astigmatism. Repeat with other eye, your*
> *neighbors and acquaintances.*

She distrusts the latter, can only imagine the response
like when she built, flew
paper planes through
the beer buzz
of dim
college
parties.

No one was amused
but herself. The psych
majors taking her
name for possible case

studies. The Optometrist explains
her penchant for receiving multiple socks
in the eye, how airborne objects could be
drawn toward her right lens, her right
lens like a football.

> *I recommend soccer. No softball, baseball . . . any ball*
> *in a lifted axis.*

And she wishes, she had known him
        back in elementary school. So many
stomachaches she wouldn't have had
        to fake. How many acts left
for the stage? The football left for her
        right eye, the eye of marked astigmatism
how not like the spontaneous
        bleeding of saints because it has an "a"
because it has an "a" it means corrective
        lenses, focus with interference, a future of being called
on in class, expected to give the right answer.

An Exploration After 6,000 mg of Amoxicillin

After she ate what felt like everything
she took to the taste of color.

        And apologized only to the Sun
for not having noticed sooner how edible
his yawns.

Even the neighbor's crayons disappeared
three by three, returning—
little nubs with lip shine, sometime after midnight.

There were rumors.

        Someone had vamped van Gogh—
unrolled his starry night, like billboard scroll
sending bicycles soaring, the road steering itself.

And she went on.

Her sampler, a sip from what once was
church, now mosque. A tulip field, spilt
stamen, pistil.

        And when she was finished,
her body, thick with theft, her tongue cut
on canvas, a train station

needle (reused)—all color bled together
and she no longer hungry, belched canals
and she no longer thirsty, wept.

Massage School Translations

for Dr. Greg Yasuda

Sometime second term you will discover your sits
        bones are *ischial tuberosities*—that every tuberosity
        is a protuberance, a process. And you will find ways

to hassle your Anatomy and Physiology
        teacher, point to your nose and claim it
        noseus process. A joke only a fellow

A+P student could enjoy. Sometime mid-second
        term you will palpate for these *ischial
        tuberosities. On yourself and a partner*

*locate these bony prominences; remember to stay
        away from the gluteal cleft.* And you will
        watch a room full of adults sitting on their

hands, some coping like cranes, one appendage
        waving for balance, another diving below
        a cheek, searching for solid underneath.

Thankfully, this will precede the construction
        men across the street, a host of workers sparking
        fire to metal. Here you rely on earth, the process

of calcification, the mutual adjustments of language
        from ass to ischial. There is a bowl in your
        pelvis, it has been there whether

you acknowledge it, it holds space
        for the *adductors* you never knew,
        a family of muscles to align you.

On an Interview to Rent Space from a Chiropractor, I Discover a Mutual Admiration for Handling Skulls

for the Benson family

He says *I'll just be*
a minute and disappears beyond
the door marked *Employees Only*.
In the room labeled *A*, I turn
to the erase board that spells
the definition of something kinetic,
as the doctor returns.

> His fingers lace
> a human skull. *Can't get these*
> *anymore*, he claims and what
> others leave, I seize.

How did you? I ask and he tells me
A religious sect in India had no problem
selling these; only problem was people left
their bodies more quickly.

I trace the parietal
suture below my finger. How young, I think
and he responds how neatly ossified, how not old and I try
not to think of family and I think of family as I speak
the tongue of sutures, what seals
bone to bone what breathes if given
space.

> He tells me
> of his daughter as he wings
> open the gates of the teeth, his daughter
> pre-med for dentistry, she will inherit
> this. It will be necessary.

We close with the orbits—a simple communion, we sip
from their thinness, tip the skull to locate light.

II.

AN ARC TOWARD NORMALCY

We Are Doing Rounds

I enter the CCU two paces behind
your suited legs, your classic loafers
squeak, remind me of the elephant

stories you'll tell before bed.
And I won't think on death,
but notice that smell I'm glad

to leave. If it had a name,
you wouldn't let me say it.
The elderly appear similarly,

their faces droop like hush
puppies. You introduce me to Mrs.
Harrison. She squeezes my hand,

says you saved her
heart, again. The man
behind the curtain

brings us chips
at Christmas, a tin
filled with salted crisps.

In the EKG lab, you value
peaks. Someone's beat charted
in ink, an arc toward normalcy.

I want to draw these people
hearts, but they always turn
out the same—

flat as valentines—
the one on your desk falls
apart, a chamber at a time.

You place it in my hands,
twist the ventricles open,
two cold lobes drop.

Once a father, the crook of his arm

becomes swing, the play structure left to oxidize.

After the heart patients clear, he swaps stethoscope

for the necklace of his daughter, stocking legs

looping his throat, as she, on his shoulders

steals second supper: curry potatoes,

basmati rice, cucumber yogurt from his plate.

One spring, he will take her to Hanuman—

watch her watch the monkeys.

When We Raise a Wall, We Leave Dixie Out

That Christmas, our father overstocked the room beside
our kitchen with boxes for the doctors,

each one, cardboard white with a cartoon
emblem in hunter green, the happy detail

of a stocking cap atop every peanut. And when
we heard the flat of Mom's sole disappearing,

we became architects
our hands the slippery

tools of reconstruction to lay
square by waxy square

along the Southern perimeter,
one uncertain tower below

our sure-fire feet and we would dip
over, pretend our legs were jelly,

elastic, something with bounce,
because we couldn't imagine a landing

without recovery, and we were too young
for the lessons of the blood-orange

flag, with the X of stars
that blew in our neighbors' yard.

In our family home we, like our mother's cuttings, will grow

under glass, sky lights shedding South-
eastern sun. And mother, we celebrate
in winter, recall 1948,
never wonder about the iron
man cast without a heart.

A Rotterdam, wasted grey
from war. An uncle plagued
by that cart of broken
bodies, always the scream
of his father, the slap
of hand to eyes too late.

And in our father's mind
there is a hushed
monarchy, a creek filled
with children during monsoon.
The neighbor like Paul Revere
rushing the village.

      Independence.
         Fallen Britain.

And though we shake
ourselves from the community
pool, and though we drench
in a heat like Muthoor,
mother will crank
the air when we reach the car
will have lemonade
prepared from a can
and words for how we dove
among strangers,
how far and fast we swam.

A Lesson on Dissection

The pigs arrived hermetically
sealed, the teacher in her standard
reversible skirt, rainbow side up.

It was not the seventies, but who
would inform her when there were
baby mammalians to prepare,

unseal and rubber band into place.
Nobody mentioned the cold trays
all shiny metal, the size

of mothers' casserole dishes.
They thought of their sweet Virginia
ham applied neat to bread.

While naming their piggies,
one employed his granddaddy's,
swearing his classmates to secrecy

as if they personally knew
Aubrey the hog farmer
somewhere North of here.

And the teacher wore a smile
pressed like a dead animal
to a pan, as the students wondered

who would unwrap her,
rub her belly with false squeals
on the other side of the rainbow.

It wasn't like we were eating the squirrels

we accidentally ran over. Those were the stories we heard about
other states, where banjo was breakfast, where ranges

of mountains conjured generations
of Confederates
                            (dead and moaning).

We were all camellia, box turtle, and the occasional
pelican. Sand between webbing, witches'

                beard for weaves, but mostly box
                stores, 5-lane highways, 35 minutes

from friends of friends who ripped the legs
off frogs two at a time to preserve

jumpability. In school (it was private)
                demerits were served
(entrée or dessert) for even thinking

                            these things.

We were raised
acorns below bicycle,
balloon between spokes,

                            the thrill of mimicry. The sound of what sounded
                            like motorcycle—buzzing like bee, like danger.

The swamp (First Landing) we explored on field
trips. Cyprus knees lifted a slick skirt, revealing

nothing but darkness, a bed for water

                            moccasin, cottonmouth—names
                            to dissolve below tongue as the myth

of anything, as though we might resurrect
something close to a dragon, not smoke-filled or bent

on bringing us closer
to Jesus the Christ

               but Jesús the foreign
                 exchange student, all picante

and lips to rival Julian whose wine
blessed us as much

as the idea of France could.
To say the swamp was the color

        of tannin would be too much when
        we didn't know what tannin was

when wine was something
to be had in mason jars, tea

        iced and artificial. We weren't

            looking for snakes or anything
            except for Robert trying to peek

        up Kathryn's skirt, which wasn't much
of a skirt—a band all sticky and time-held—a watch

        that went on ticking with the pulse
        of what kept the boys calibrated, close.

We didn't think.

We were young, we were the South risen, continuing to rise.

The Cardiologist's daughter contemplates a heart

breaking open, four chambers
           of blood, bed clothes spooling red
           rain or one scissor

      kick, an organ attempting AWOL.
      She knows enough
to know these things

happen, the healthy spouse
      collapsing days after
           the beloved. She's seen

      the graves.
      When will science
learn what her father knows—

the heart is a house
      tended with dream, it gives in
           when it wishes.

Eight Years After, Pink Still Startles Her

In memory of Mrs. Anne Grinnell

Because the coffin was the color of cotton
    candy before it's spun

Because her hands were still puckered
    from morning bath

Because the congregation swelled
    into a uniform flesh

Because her mother's marriage gown was one
    shade lighter than the casket

Because this wasn't her birth
    mother but close enough

Because the box didn't glide but
    snagged on her dress

Because the pushcart wheels
    bled a trail of rust

Because even the preacher
    would cry

III.

Eulogy For Collapsed Structures

Cranberry Sauce Provides an Improper Dressing
for the Modern Turkey

One day post-Thanksgiving my mother delivers a eulogy
for collapsed structures.

The balcony splinters, turns away
from the bedroom, approaches the formal

living room below, while my father inside, waits
for his arteries to narrow.

The study of hearts only instructs
so much. How to mend

a pumping mass, preserve
what will not keep.

My mother wraps, unwraps
leftovers, addresses each dish with a dose

of plastic sheathing. Days ago, a miniature balloon
inside my father bellowed. And I arrived

at the understanding that we wouldn't be taking this balloon
ride together, or one with hot air, a basket

attached for human voyage. What constricts, dilates.

What empties, fills.

The Cardiologist Speaks

I traded mango trees for the ripeness
of D.C. in spring.

Retrained my voice
to lose my Malayalam accent,

retrained myself to be the medical
model. Allopathic. The sole trace

of India, my skin. On Connecticut
Avenue, I shared a flat with an extended family

of cockroaches, the never-ending
tale of the tenant in 14-A who swallowed

one, how he awoke to the sound
of crunching—his jaw operating solo.

In the hospital, it was worse. 36-hour
shifts and the tea never strong enough

—no one knew to boil the water twice—
I had to bring my own loose leaf

delivered from a friend of a friend of a family
member from Kerala. Everyone here drank

coffee, the kind that makes you shake
the kind that could be dangerous while conducting

medical procedures. For years, I was monitored.
Rules, regulations fastened to me like the ECG

pads I adhered to my patients' chests. I learned
how to palpate the pulse of the hospital,

to translate what I knew from what was missing
in their eyes—why I would order another test, when

to follow code. They would not believe me if I shared
what I found, so much longing misread for failure.

The Language of Fire

First abandon your ears; fire does not speak in raised tones
like some choral director or toddler, his indoor voice creeping
when mother exits the room.

Picture your father at the edge
of the jungle, his path shortest through vine

his mother's warning words
Mon, take the long way home.

If he does not listen, strides past
the dozing cobra, will the tongue of fire strike

or rest coiled? At night when men
complain of chest pain, women of aching

above brow-line
fire dips her robes in ochre, her figure
a shadow, rushes you.

In America, Auntie remembers Janaki

for Indira Auntie

while passing a toy store with stuffed snakes, felt tongues

and plastic eyes—nothing like where Janaki prays.

Here children worship animals from factories.

Bodies similar in smell, touch. No difference

between monkey, tiger or the lime-green crocodile.

Inhaling, Janaki wends her way to Temple,

her faith spread between golden

and rat snakes, placed firmly in each viper's

ability to puncture and spew.

—Children in New Jersey have no need for stillness,

their reptiles remain frozen in descent—

Exhaling, Janaki calms her thought, body

does not fear the open window, does not fear

the snake lying before the altar.

Still, Auntie hastens, leaves American children tempting

creatures to fall, Janaki to a world of prayer among poison.

In Dream We Support a Two-Headed Tiger

i.

Your lap, my hands the bolsters—we hold

this Bengal, this vanilla
coat with stripes, this two-headed creature

whose breath could melt coconuts, whose eyes
would trance the staunchest of priests.

We do not speak.
And the circle around us is hush—

hush like a church before psalm, a cult
before initiates. They and you appear

as one. And I do not belong
here, I realize my hold.

Where a belly should be, a second
set of teeth snaps.

ii.

You wake to mangos, the feeling
of clay below you—an ache
in the groin.   In my sleep, you still
                         cradle a cat, your lap weighing down, down.

Here, Padmini, your lotus
girl sings in Hindi—

                    you take your morning
                    meal with your mother, her mother—
                    your hands, a color wheel of savory.

From below the table, your daughter roars
and you recall—*Last night I dreamt of strangers*
coarse as salt from the Rann.

iii.

The circle is not a church but a flame, a sodium
bright flame in which you begin

to sing and we walk through fire
like it is normal as the two-headed tiger

we become, our skins made
deep with stripes.

How We Sketch the Departed

In memory of A.G. Boxman

i.

That night the butterfly scorched

in the woodstove due to inattention, mine

and the butterfly's. Flame sputtered as smoke

formed a pillow for the insect's final sleep—black

smearing the azure that lined its wings.

And I did not know the sound of butterfly

trapped in fire—the beat against current, the pop

of madrona against wing.

And the butterfly

gone blacker than any butterfly in nature, puffed

its wings as if to fly but froze instead, its body thin as rice

paper in my palm, its heat a slight singe.

ii.

I come from a clan of butterfly

watchers, not deaf to the turn

of Swallowtail

not unaware of what the dark

butterfly brings.

I can close my eyes

and feel blood, the flutter

of ventricles dipping their wings.

iii.

My family carries roses to the sea

and pine switches, sliced

from our Christmas tree, its skirt

of boughs—shortened

to honor Father, Grandfather, a man

who commanded thousands

of conifers for his Dutch nursery

and my brother breaks

the crust of the earth

delivers my mother's candle

shores up the candle

with sand, a small

flame before wave

and they practice

letting go, one

at a time

when a rose returns, my aunt

returns it, her arm the arc

of what my mother remembers—

my father, me, her sprig

three roses, red, she releases

and from her palm, a trail

of phosphorescence

her body to sea.

iv.

I smell the earth; it is thick with rain.

On my altar a dragonfly wing

I hold beneath my grandfather's image—

pin it with stone, some smoky

quartz. It is early winter, between Mourning

and Long Nights Moon. I sacrifice nothing

but wood and paper. I draw white

butterflies on white paper, wait for the moon

to acid-test my sketch, already slipping.

To Draw, To Smoke

for Oom Hendrik

After a season of war
he drew with charcoal.

Fire shooting from his fingers—
first his country colors.

Regal orange, like the House
of Orange and blue deep
as Delft canals.

        Pastels
pilfered from the art
academy.

      A lone chariot
appearing across the page
over, over, the outline
smudged.

     Flame cradled the wheels, held them within
boundary while the stallion—spooked—bucked,
its mane, a whirl.

The repetition of what burns.

       Blauw. Oranje.

      And he could not release
that cart from memory—the loose
braid of corpses—pigments

in his palette he would toss.
No more scarlet or dirt
brown. Just scavenged stubs

orange and blue like some
plant in a smoldering city—
its flower, paradise.

Kneeling to Ganges

Already past the hundred mark, the temperature
is set to rise. The funeral pyre arranged, awaits

the oldest nephew for the original fire
rite. And they say it will not smell.

The final passing: flesh to flame, hair to wind,
bones to ground. Sandalwood, a crackle below

Uncle. No one will cover an eye to the Gods.
Auntie, not cloaked in her wedding sari, not jeweled

or scented for sati. See how Nephew circles dear
Uncle, taps his crown with a staff-like switch, invites

his spirit to flee. Soon they will dip temples
of prayer, saffron flowers into the Ganges, worship

the Great Mother with illumination.

As In Dutch, As In You

It takes twenty-eight years plus three hundred and fifty five days to learn enough
about your family, understand the great uncle beyond his hair, always swooped
in half-figure eight, those trademark eyes glacial even in black and white.

Before your mother unwound with disease, her father's ashes released
who would discuss the War, detail every eldest son whose name
was Henk. Unphotographed years posit in your mother's shoulders,

her brother's upper hunch, the everything that was never
discussed at dinner, why butterflies are messengers remembered
from torture chambers, their inscription the lesson for your grandfather's

brothers who made their bodies slight as insect for escape.
And how the women, the wives vanished, their children
packed for the country, worry ushered like kerchief

underneath sleeve or daring between breasts. No wonder
your grandfather trusted a sharp blade, the first push from bank,
the cinnamon whirl from windmill on the opposite side of the lake.

Now, by the waters too warm to freeze, your mother speaks
and speaks, unbinds the skein behind her father's collection
of antique skates—here a host of reasons to keep the family

sealed in a bed of ice.

Reading My Mother's Words on the Path to My Cabin

And then the chimney came down and the house was thrown into the trash.

There is no introduction
this card speaks
      like an overturned Bible.

And I know I am missing
something, so I slow
      down, churn the passage

like cream. Let memory
uncoil her flaxen
      tresses until I see

the house built fresh
from ginger cookies
      a chimney caving

weeks after Christmas.
And still, my brother's
      sums of the right

triangle, the roof
that failed us
      in everything but theory—

lie flat on the notepad
by Mother's phone.
      But the house

it stood like any ranch
in January, a horizontal
      catching snow

to stucco until time
(that little bastard)
      could not wait

any longer, slid himself
from below, his birth
      the quick choke.

IV.

Somewhere in a Room of Eggs

The Cardiologist, his daughter cradle a model

skull—they've left hearts behind years ago for osteo-

      cytes, sutures: sagittal, coronal—

sockets whose purpose is stationary

grace, how to hold what fills

      how to balance what adheres.

The Cardiologist, his daughter love to learn

      the language of mater: dura,

      arachnoid, pia—whisper

the sound CSF

      would make if it were

external, how not

rapid but river

      one flow sub-

      dividing.

After the tsunami, we searched

December 26, 2004

     for an open line for days while no one

phoned. It was nearly New Year's.

     My father perched glasses

         upon his face, scooched so near

the TV as though he might seize

     the woman in the maroon sari, plunge

         his arms into the Sony, draw

her through the light

     of the screen.

It was an annual ritual—

     alms for the sea.

     Everywhere devotees

offering sweetmeats, promises

of loyalty.

In our home, the remnants of Christmas

a tree glowing with miniature

    white. My mother fed us

        leftovers, the smell of mushrooms ascended

        cradled the silence that no one wanted—

           Our family—too early

               for the boatman—too late

they traded the shore

for a car   fleeing the wave   the size of a God   herself.

And still, we remain

we remain still.

The Cardiologist's daughter is concerned

with needles, the thought of what keeps

blood fixed—what accounts
for system failure, a heart spilling—

what blurs on screen
a mitral valve prolapsing.

She learns to mind
adjusts to right side

reduces intake of sugar
caffeine. The Cardiologist's daughter

feels so much, removes
tags from sweaters

will not stand anything approaching
her throat—remembers the time

when D. slapped a bee clear
into her back—the sting

she had never felt
before, nothing

like needle, more like twinge.
The instructor not believing

her calmness, taking
ten minutes to notice

stinger through flesh.
The Cardiologist's daughter

is complicated. She has a thing
for discovery, keeps a collection

including the bear
claw, countless bones,

something potentially human.
She would have the complete

skeleton, if she could afford—
She has made peace

with weird, has a pink
dot on her ID, sees

herself on that metal
table while waiting

at checkouts—those tabloids—
so less appealing. Called

morbid, she cannot help
a family that served

obituaries with cornflakes
longer than she has been drinking

her coffee near black.
She fills herself with herself

as a baker would install a pie
with nectarine—there are places

where the color blurs and she forgets
outer for inner. They call

her edgy and she says I am
regardless, concentrated with core.

After My Mother's Hip Replacement
We Gather Around Her Heart

Before the lamp, my father lifts
the film, points to what appears

to be ivy looping over the branches
of my mother's heart.

        He hands me my mother's heart
indicates where the bird's beak

was—has vanished. No more
nesting near valve

only the supposition—
how one radiologist declared

        my mother's heart
had wings or beak.

He wanted her
to have something

that would open, tend her
while the cardinals winter

        away. I offer hair—
my own fallen—fistfuls

I collect to match my father's
so she might build

        from her daughter's
cells, dismiss the rumor

of beak—remember the raptor
who returns, never opens his throat—

only focuses on what below reveals.

When I Approach my Advisor for Advice on How to Move Forward With Greater Ease After a Bumpy Start of Going Pre-Med in My Thirties, He Performs a Well-Rehearsed Soliloquy

Every year there are those who fall.
He draws me a curve—

epinephrine on the x, performance on the y.
A straight line to the top where some—

he references me—go over.
I imagine the remains,

the class of forty trimmed
extra length in the row below

the Periodic Table, the ease with which
legs stretch in the presence of space.

He has never performed surgery,
never cleaved anything but a hypothetical

student from the breast of Post-Bacc
status, never attended

himself, but he is an expert
of probability. Vex one student

and observe wilt under scrutiny.
Take three quizzes and don't call me.

I would bottle it if I could—he speaks
of success, those shy of adrenaline

junkies—*I would be rich.*
I think of my father with only three

dollars upon immigrating. Practicing in his native
country, the requirement of redoing his residency—

the subsequent years of specializing, cardiology.
My father thinks of me, my advisor thinks.

After Completing the MCAT and Before Returning
to the Northwest, My Room Fills with Longing

for Matt Cummings

It wasn't Amsterdam, but you rode without
helmet through the streets of Oakland

all the way to Alameda, where
the dams of everything I held

threatened to overflow
through each open window

that kept the heat
from catching my linens

on fire—the loft
walls with Southern

exposure not the sole cause
of combustion, still the principle

with whatever string of monomers
linked to form the mattress foam

too close to something
spontaneous—

but this wasn't a physical
emergency—nothing leaping

at my bed
and you

arrived to collect
whatever I had

the medical college
admissions texts never

highlighted yet searched
for potential—you

gathered me
from every direction

packed those plastics full with garments
the vacuum cleaner reducing excess

oxygen—more space
for me to leave.

When asked what you know about grief, you remind me

of me—that I don't believe in umbrellas

or eggs or beets or anything

that could pass for an egg,

an umbrella, a beet.

You tell me there is a meadow beyond

the fence over there and how it disappeared

your dog—but that fence is falling,

has been in a perpetual state

of suspension since you and I have—

and you are allergic to fur.

You are in the middle of an omelet

without ketchup, only because there isn't,

and you tell me grief is like this

as you point to your plate and I agree.

When asked what you know

you tell me of a field above a hill

below a trail that keeps expanding,
how you never approached

the ocean, only collected
advances as others weeds.

You tell me the trail leads
no one. You remind me

of what migrates.
I remind you of wind

how it holds the red-tail
steady. You say current

is current, treading
inevitable—we are

featherless, our legs
relinquish. If you find

the barn empty where
the red finch sings,

if you find yourself
sudden as hunger—

There Are Times When the Heart Stops and the Person Continues

This may sound simple but stop—

There is more than cell death, the subsequent shock for return

Put aside the yogis who may will their organs still

I am right here and you are somewhere in a room of eggs

And someone right now is stopping—I can feel the strong glaze

Even this distance is nothing (when compared to matters of the heart)

There are ways in which we shutter

Another loved becomes obsolete, we no longer receive him

for undetermined or determined reasons he is no more

or no more present in a room of eggs than in a field

of windmills We continue, our lungs breathe us

one inspiration after another but our hearts

stop We present ourselves in Chemistry, conduct

experiments involving the sublimation of caffeine

watch the corresponding development of crystals—perfect

diminutive icicles—upon a cold finger

We are not thinking about the process of respiration

but notice the chill of extraction

My Feeling for Stab Lab is Like a Left to Right Shunt Progressing to a Right to Left Shunt, Something that Requires Attention Before Potential Cyanosis

i.

If I told you my first
was with a butterfly

that it took three
times, before I could

stick. The instructor
priming me with

What will it take?

and I couldn't answer
to failure. But the flash

that followed, far
more electric than

anything I had ever—
a steady crimson

filling a tiger
top. The shock

of placing a 23
G with accuracy

the unexpected
heat of letting—

ii.

In this chapter, I discover
the key between precision

and accuracy. I am zero
for four and I skipped

a night of ferries (and you)
for hours upon

hours of precisely
missing the median

cubital, some lovely
part of a dorsal

venous network
that likes to shake

it to the left while
my anchor retreats.

I am reminded
this isn't metaphor.

I follow anything
but an apparent aqua-

marine as I coin
the term invisi-

vein, retract my
needle and leave.

iii.

Here you may find yourself
disappointed—

I thought you would know what you're doing.

Here is where I wish I believed
in sports other than hockey

to give you some sweet stat
rather than a puck in the face.

iv.

May I wow you with my delivery—
a one-two butterfly syringe drawing 5 mL
from the hand of the one we call bloodless.

Laughter—the previously unknown
trick of dilation—and that one errant
freckle. I recommend you hang a right.

In January   Our Rib Cages Are Cleaved

for Dr. Love

Then there is the moment   when we are asked

to open   our palms   curl

    our fingers

            to receive   what   skipped

       operated with   impulse   solely

            to accept   this

            collection

            of cells   once

         examined   below   scope

      would appear striated   but not   just

      striated   specialized

        this organ   of pulse

        and organ   ization

     this synergist   of breath

a muscle   of varying   mass

with   which   desire   was

          implied   volumes   read

between   an inner   most

smooth   a novel   of

          unending   until

                    the moment   before
                    the moment   before now

NOTES:

"The Acupuncturist warns the Cardiologist's daughter" is dedicated to Denise DuPree, LAc, fellow cardio daughter.

"We speak of water" is dedicated to Ilya Kaminsky.

The title "We leave the beaches for the tourists, mostly" was taken from the 2007 Tupelo Press poetry prompts. On September 3, 2001, two tourists swimming off the Outer Banks, NC were attacked by a shark. The man was pronounced dead and the woman survived. This poem draws from this event.

"Massage School Translations" is dedicated to Dr. Greg Yasuda.

"On an Interview to Rent Space from a Chiropractor, I Discover a Mutual Admiration for Handling Skulls" is dedicated to the Benson family.

In "Once a father, the crook of his arm" Hanuman refers to the Hindu monkey deity and to the broader concept of Hanuman. When visiting India with my father, I begged him to bring me to a monkey temple. While the Chamakkavu Devi temple in Chengannur (Kerala, India) is not considered a Hanuman temple, wild monkeys, along with the occasional escaped zoo monkey, populate the grounds.

"In our family home we, like our mother's cuttings, will grow" *The iron man cast without a heart* refers to Ossip Zadkine's WWII sculpture "De Verwoeste Stad" (The Destroyed City), a memorial for May 14, 1940 when German Nazis razed Rotterdam to the ground. Muthoor refers to my father's hometown in Kerala, India.

"Eight Years After, Pink Still Startles Her" is dedicated to the memory of Mrs. Anne Grinnell.

"The Language of Fire" *Mon* is a term of endearment used for a son in Malayalam (the language of Kerala, India).

"In America, Auntie remembers Janaki" is dedicated to Indira Auntie and to the memory of my grandmother, Janaki.

"In Dream We Support a Two-Headed Tiger" *The Rann* refers to the Rann of Kutch salt marshes located in Gujarat (West India). The salt workers, due to their high salt content, are known for not decomposing completely during cremation.

"How We Sketch the Departed" is dedicated to the memory of my Opa (Grandfather) A.G. Boxman.

"To Draw, To Smoke" is dedicated to my Oom (Uncle) Hendrik Boxman.

"Kneeling to Ganges" is dedicated to my Indian family. It is written with the hope that India, as a nation, moves away from the practice of sati versus just the enforcement of law. Sati: the act whereby a widow willingly or unwillingly enters the funeral pyre with her husband's burning body.

"As In Dutch, As In You" is dedicated to my Dutch family. In particular, this poem is for my Opa and great uncles who served in the Resistance in WWII, all of whom escaped from the clutch of German Nazis and/or concentration camps.

"After the tsunami, we searched" is dedicated to my Indian family, specifically those relatives who escaped with a slim margin that day and in memory of the approximate 300,000 lost.

"After Completing the MCAT and Before Returning to the Northwest, My Room Fills with Longing" is dedicated to Matt Cummings.

"My Feeling for Stab Lab is Like a Left to Right Shunt Progressing to a Right to Left Shunt, Something that Requires Attention Before Potential Cyanosis" is dedicated to those who offered me their veins.

"In January   Our Rib Cages Are Cleaved " is dedicated to Dr. Love.

Natasha Kochicheril Moni is a first-generation American of Dutch and East Indian descent. She completed her BA in Child Development at Tufts University, premedical education at Mills College, and is a naturopathic medical student at Bastyr University.

Born in the North and raised in the South, Natasha finds home in the Pacific Northwest. Here, her funny little habits of collecting model hearts, skulls, feathers, and miscellaneous bones are tolerated (generally). She feels fortunate to sip on a glass of red to the background of the Olympic Mountains—to be within walking distance from the Puget Sound, and to be in community with cutting-edge writers and health care practitioners, alike.

Her poetry, fiction, essays, and reviews have been published in over fifty journals, recognized in competitions, and awarded her a Puffin Foundation grant. More of Natasha's work and musings may be found on her site/blog: www.natashamoni.com

Publications by Two Sylvias Press:

The Daily Poet: Day-By-Day Prompts For Your Writing Practice
by Kelli Russell Agodon and Martha Silano (Print and eBook)

Fire On Her Tongue: An Anthology of Contemporary Women's Poetry
edited by Kelli Russell Agodon and Annette Spaulding-Convy (Print and eBook)

The Poet Tarot and Guidebook: A Deck Of Creative Exploration (Print)

The Cardiologist's Daughter
by Natasha Kochicheril Moni (Print and eBook)

She Returns to the Floating World
by Jeannine Hall Gailey (Print and eBook)

Hourglass Museum
by Kelli Russell Agodon (eBook)

Dear Alzheimer's: A Caregiver's Diary & Poems
by Esther Altshul Helfgott (eBook)

Listening to Mozart: Poems of Alzheimer's
by Esther Altshul Helfgott (eBook)

Cloud Pharmacy
by Susan Rich (eBook)

Crab Creek Review 30th Anniversary Issue featuring Northwest Poets
edited by Kelli Russell Agodon and Annette Spaulding-Convy (eBook)

Please visit Two Sylvias Press (www.twosylviaspress.com) for information on purchasing our print books, eBooks, writing tools, and for submission guidelines for our annual chapbook prize. Two Sylvias Press also offers editing services and manuscript consultations.

Created with the belief that great writing
is good for the world.

two sylvias press

Visit us online: www.twosylviaspress.com

Praise for *The Cardiologist's Daughter*

Natasha Moni is the poet who comes to us "from the clan of the butterfly watchers." I love her poems in this book. I suggest you open it to a poem such as "As In Dutch, As In You" or her sequence of the "Cardiologist's daughter" and you will find a voice which is able to find lyric in moments of each day, to find music in medicine, to find strange clarity in each of us. This is a beautiful debut. —Ilya Kaminsky, author of *Dancing in Odessa*

This doctor's daughter sings of the literal as well as the figurative heart, in poems that are haunting and elegiac. Moni's love of the language of medicine and anatomy, as well as a deep respect for her Indian and Dutch family roots, are evident throughout these delightful poems. Though her life path may evolve differently than her Cardiologist father's, they both bend toward healing as art. —Peter Pereira, author of *Saying the World*

Natasha Moni writes with unflinching honesty and subtle surprise. *The Cardiologist's Daughter* is both cryptic and conversational, self-deprecating and transcendent—a tender homage to her Indian and Dutch family roots and an intense reflection on the quest for personal identity. —Anjali Banerjee, author of *Haunting Jasmine* and *Enchanting Lily*

Made in the USA
San Bernardino, CA
18 February 2016